TOTTERDOWN

1. Bath Bridge on the main road from central Bristol to Totterdown and Knowle. This view in 1911 looking towards Victoria Street and the city The Castle and Plough Inn on the corner of Clarence Road has since been demolished and a second bridge built to the left of the original.

2. Bath road repair shop. Picture taken on the 4th July 1947 showing 3300 Bulldog class 4 4 0 Engine, Penguin. Built at Swindon about 1900 and based at Swindon in 1948.

TOTTERDOWN

3. Horse drawn tram on the Bath Road side of the Three Lamps. These trams were first introduced into Bristol on August 9th 1875 and from 1879 plied their trade from Bristol Bridge to Three Lamps, and on the Bath road to Arnos Vale 1898. The first Electric Trams having been introduced on the 1st February 1897.

4. The junction of Bath and Wells Roads, in 1911, showing shops and properties on the left and a man working on the roof, with many advertising hoardings on the Wells road side.

TOTTERDOWN

5. The Three Lamps, practically a traffic jam! Tram No. 220 travelling from Brislington to Hotwells, while No.89 is travelling to Knowle, one passenger just reaching the top deck and No.72 is on its way to Bristol Bridge.

6. A different type of transport is shown in this picture. Four legged horses power! The Three Lamps signpost can be seen under the sign advertising Rogers Pale Ale, with the white hand pointing the way to Bath. George Fear watchmaker & jeweller had the shop on the corner, where a drinking fountain is also situated.

TOTTERDOWN

7. This view of the Three Lamps was taken in 1920. The whole area is completely changed today. Both Wells Road and Bath Road have been widened, all the buildings in the picture have been demolished, and the wall on the right of the picture has been cut back. But one familiar object has been restored, the Three Lamps Standard.

8. Bath Road in 1911, the turning on the right is Angers Road, with the Turnpike Inn centre of the picture. The houses on the hill, leading to Totterdown, can be approached by Thunderbolt Steps. The elegant terraced houses, backing onto the river were demolished for road widening.

TOTTERDOWN

9. Further along Bath Road, with County Street turning off to the right. An interesting advertising sign, a barrel hanging from a hoist.

10. St. Mary Redcliffe cemetery opposite Arnos Vale in about 1910. Interesting combination of advertisements on the wall of the house. Van Houtens Cocoa above G. Tuckfield & Co., with G. Greenaway, Monumental Sculptors below.

TOTTERDOWN

11. The imposing Identical Lodges each side of the gateway of Arnos Vale Cemetery. Known as Bristol Cemetery when first opened in the mid 1800s.

12. Inside the Cemetery, the steep path to the Nonconformist Chapel. The church of England Chapel not in view, but situated to the left of the gates. This picture postcard posted in 1910.

TOTTERDOWN

13. The main shopping area of Totterdown known as the "Bush", after the Bush Hotel on the corner with Bush Street in this view in 1905. The shop on the right, W. Goodall and Sons, was noted for home-made Boots and Shoes. Tram 67 travelling from Knowle to Joint Railway Station and Bristol Bridge.

14. Totterdown Linen Warehouse, owned by Fosters, their extensive shop on the left hand side of Wells Road below the junction with St. Johns Lane, in the direction of the city. Postcard postally used in 1908.

TOTTERDOWN

15. Wells Road looking towards Knowle from St. Johns Lane, the prominent building of Totterdown Y.M.C.A. on the corner of Bushy Park postally used in 1907. The shop in the left hand corner of the picture advertises "Hair cutting, Shampooing and Shaving Rooms" and the cart belongs to D.M.W. Bullock & Co., mineral waters.

16. This bustling view on the bend at the "Bush" shows shoppers walking in the road, and boarding trams in both directions in about 1914. Hodders the Chemist is on the left of the picture.

TOTTERDOWN

17. The same junction of Wells Road in 1920. Tram No.67, with destination board No.10, was introduced in 1913. The tram is en route from Knowle to the Joint Railway Station (Temple Meads) and Bristol Bridge.

18. Another view from outside the Bush Hotel in about 1933. A telephone box and litter bin are much in evidence, a sign of progress! Tram No. 197 is on Route 15, Hanham – Old Market – Bushy Park (later extended to Knowle).

TOTTERDOWN

19. Bushy Park Wesleyan Chapel in the road of that name before 1910. Today it is Totterdown Methodist Chapel, a thriving community church.

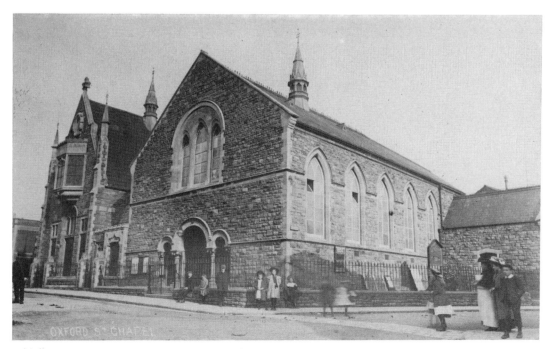

20. Oxford Street Chapel, a Methodist church built in 1874. It was situated between Bush Street and Cheapside Street, and demolished in the 1970s.

TOTTERDOWN

21. St. Lukes Road from the St. Johns Lane end, in about 1910. Beyond the Cumberland Hotel on the right is Windsor Terrace, and further down on the left hand side is Hill Avenue. The houses in the centre of the picture have been demolished and the road widened to the edge of Victoria Park.

22. Totterdown from Victoria Park, showing the terraced streets towards Bushy Park. The fields were later transformed with houses in Ravenhill Road etc. and Perretts Park. The open air baths can be seen on the left of the picture, the "Deep End" clearly visible.

TOTTERDOWN

23. Ascending the hill from Bushy Park towards Knowle, an advertisement for Snowball Patent Flour on the end wall of the rank of shops and just below on the right, by the group of people on the pavement, the corner of Knowle Road. Harris & Tozer drapers were on the left of the picture.

24. Looking back down Wells Road, from Holy Nativity Church by School Road, this view shows shops mixed with gabled houses.

TOTTERDOWN

25. Totterdown was home to many railway workers, with its close proximity to Temple Meads Station. This picture shows a G.W.R. railway guard and his family outside their home at 20 William Street, Totterdown.

26. A view looking towards the Bush from Firfield Street, with the Totterdown Hotel on the corner of County Street. The blinds of shops in Oxford Street can be seen near the Methodist Chapel (See picture no.20). The old shops have been demolished, the Bush Hotel rebuilt, also a new housing complex.

TOTTERDOWN

Holy Nativity, Totterdown, Bristol. 194

27. The Church of Holy Nativity was dedicated September 14th 1871. This view taken before the tower was built, which was added in 1931. The church was destroyed in the blitz in 1940 and the Parochial Hall was fitted out as a church and used from August 1941. The church was rebuilt and re-consecrated 25th January 1958.

28. The interior of Holy Nativity church showing the double patterned curve of the roof, looking towards the high altar. This postcard was postally used in August 1924.

29. Outside Holy Nativity Church crowds gathered to witness the funeral procession of Rev. H de C Wingfield on February 22nd 1913. He was appointed vicar to the church in 1905.

30. The funeral cortege wending its way up Wells Road, after the funeral service, passing the houses above the Baptist Church.

TOTTERDOWN

31. Wells Road, Tram No. 69 travelling from Knowle and just passing Holy Nativity Church en route for Bristol Bridge. This card postally used September 1920.

32. Haverstock Road, a turning on the right off of the Wells Road, it crosses Fairfoot Road and connects with Bayham Road at the far end.

TOTTERDOWN

Wells Rd. Totterdown, from Knowle.

No. 105.

33. Looking towards Totterdown from Knowle, by the turning with Clyde Road. Postally used in 1904, this is a view easily recognised today with the trees very much in evidence.

Wells Road Baptist Chapel, Totterdown, Bristol.

34. Wells Road Baptist Chapel on the corner of Cemetery Road and Sydenham Road. The church notice board is announcing the coming Harvest Festival in September 1906.

35. Brecknock Road from Bayham Road looking towards Wells road, in 1923.

36. Brecknock Road looking in the opposite direction, showing open fields beyond. This postcard was sent as a personal Christmas Greetings card from No.9 Brecknock Road.

37. Another view looking towards Totterdown from Clyde Road *(see also illustration no.33)*. This picture taken about 1920 shows many of the houses now converted to shops. The delivery van by the Tram advertising Mackays Herbal Tablets, and it has an early Bristol Registration No. A E 8260.

38. Looking down Wells Road in 1907, the trees newly planted, the turning on the left Rookery Road.

KNOWLE

39. The main Wells Road about 1910, the cyclist just passing the turning for Belluton Road. On the open ground behind the trees houses have now been built.

40. Belluton Road showing the large double bay villas in this view in 1923. This picture is taken from Bayham Road, and at the far end can be seen the cottages and roof and tower of the George Inn in Wells Road.

41. Wells Road. The caption reads "George Hill", but it is Wells Road and inference is to the George Inn on the corner with Somerset Road. This early view from 1906.

42. The same view of the George Inn in 1918. Tram No. 208 travelling towards the city, with a conductress on the running board. Many women were employed on Bristol's trams during the first World War.

KNOWLE

Beaconsfield Rd. Knowle.

43. Beaconsfield Road in 1907. Situated on the left hand side of Wells Road, just above the George Inn, and connecting with Harrowdene Road.

Beaconsfield Road. Knowle. 593.   York Series

44. Beaconsfield Road taken from the same corner in 1924, a busy view in the winter sunshine.

45. Harrowdene Road in 1924, showing the New Bible Christian Chapel. On the corner of Cleeve Road is the Knowle Supply Store.

46. Showing the complete frontage of the chapel, in about 1905, it has long since been demolished and houses built on the ground.

KNOWLE

47. Glena Avenue connects with Greenmore Road, and at the other end Priory Road. Priory Road joins Wells Road at the crossroads with Broad Walk. A view taken in 1912.

48. Cleeve Road is a steep road as this picture suggests, the trees newly planted. It joins with Somerset Road round the left hand bend. This postcard was postally used in 1905.

ROBERT COLE

TENOR

Triple Gold Medalist.

WINNER OF VARIOUS
CHALLENGE TROPHIES

-:-

Oratorio
Grand Opera
Concerts and Dinners.

-:-

For Terms etc.—

**134, SYLVIA AVENUE,
LOWER KNOWLE,
BRISTOL 3.**

49. The advertising postcard of Mr. Robert Cole offering his services as a tenor. for concerts etc. The postcard was sent by him to a Mr. Parry, about a coming performance to be held on September 2nd in Knowle.

50. Councillor C.R. Perrett, no doubt at the opening ceremony of Perretts Park, named after him as he contributed £500 of the £1,000 needed by Bristol Council to purchase the land for a park, in 1923. The roads bordering the park are Sylvia Avenue, Bayham Road and Ravenhill Road. This event took place in 1929.

KNOWLE

Wells Rd. Knowle. Looking South.

No. 106.

51. Wells Road looking south towards Broad Walk. The large double bay house is today Cleeve House School. This view in 1905, before building development opposite.

Greetings

52. This large detached house, one of several of similar design between Beaconsfield Road and Marston Road, is called Victoria Lodge and is no. 262, Wells Road. The postcard was posted locally at Totterdown in 1905.

53. A later view looking along the main road, with a close up view of the elegant double bay villa on the left which is now Cleeve House School. The houses opposite are now built, and Woodridge Road is completed.

54. Wells Road Schools in 1908, bordered by Greenmore Road to the left, and Maxie Road to the right. Children and mothers with young babies in their prams are in the foreground. Note the lacy canopy on one of the prams.

KNOWLE

55. Wells Road looking North, going towards the city in 1905. The cottages on the right are now converted to shops. Beyond the bay windows of the Talbot Inn, with the sign above advertising Georges Ale and Stout, can be seen the blinds of several shops.

56. Tram No. 214 passing the turning for Redcatch Road, the Wesleyan Chapel on the corner and opposite by the rank of shops is Greenmore Road.

KNOWLE

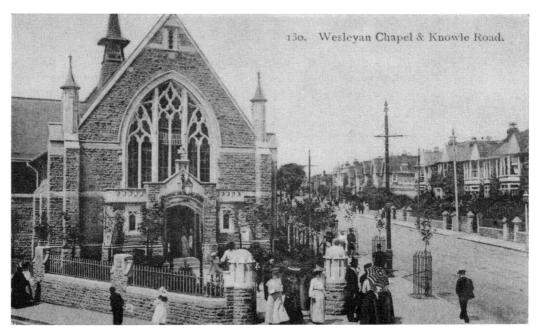

57. The Wesleyan Chapel, no doubt a Sunday, the congregation just leaving after the service. The ladies can be seen with their long skirts, large hats and umbrellas on this postcard sent from Knowle in 1908.

58. Another view of the Chapel on the corner of Redcatch Road. This view is 9 years later than illustration no. 57, in 1917. The houses to the left are in Oakmeade Park.

House of Charity, Knowle.

59. The House of Charity showing the extensive buildings of the convent in St. Agnes Avenue, sadly soon to be sold.

C 6183   CONVENT OF THE SISTERS OF CHARITY, BRISTOL. 4.

60. The front of the main building of the convent. A nun receiving visitors at the main door, a place of peace and tranquility.

61. In the garden of the convent two nuns attending the garden in this delightful springtime view.

62. The Wardens Lodge and Vicarage. These buildings within the convent complex, were converted in 1980 for use as St. Peters Hospice. An extension has since been built and the Lodge is now used as a day centre and administration block. Situated on the corner of Tennis Road and Redcatch Road, this early card was postally used in 1906.

63. Talbot Road, the turning by the cart next to the Talbot Inn. On the opposite side are three storied shops. A bustling view taken in 1924.

64. Redcatch Road looking towards the main Wells Road. The wall and trees of the Wesleyan Chapel on the left, with the shops opposite. Trading names were A. Derrick, Lester, and J. Hatcher. Two gentlemen in their "Whites" off to play Tennis or Cricket!

65. The Talbot Inn was a coaching inn when Knowle was part of Bedminster, and outside the city. This view in 1906, shops now replace the cottages.

66. Another early view in the same period as illustration no. 65, before 1910 showing the Talbot Inn with flowers in window boxes. The houses in the distance face Knowle Cricket Ground.

KNOWLE

67. Knowle Tennis Courts situated on part of the cricket ground. The postcard was written in 1906, their message reads "the tennis courts newly built".

68. Three shops, with their own front door. The first shop is Knowle Post Office, with adverts for Brooks Dye Works, and a Telegraph Office sign by the window. This postcard was sent as a greetings card in 1905.

KNOWLE

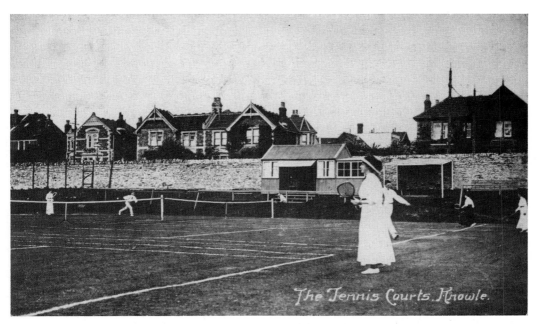

69. A view of the Tennis courts, games in progress. Note the fashions of the lady players! The space behind the pavilion, centre picture, is Priory Road showing how the tennis courts extended into what is now a widened Broad Walk. Postcard postally used in 1913.

70. The St. Johns Ambulance Brigade. Their Totterdown section in an event and demonstration on a part of Knowle Cricket and Tennis field. The houses behind the banner, on the left corner of Priory Road, now house a doctors surgery and Broad Walk has cut through this part of the field.

KNOWLE

71. The house called "Woodleigh", is No. 328 Wells Road, on the corner with Priory Road. This view dates from before 1914.

72. Broad Walk, c. 1935, with the cricket ground and tennis courts on the left. The shops on the corner included the bungalow fish and chip shop, and although the whole corner was redeveloped as a shopping complex in the 1970s, the lower shops from Smith Pram and Toy shop are still trading. A G.W.R. lorry can be seen in front of what was Smiths the Ironmongers Warehouse.

KNOWLE

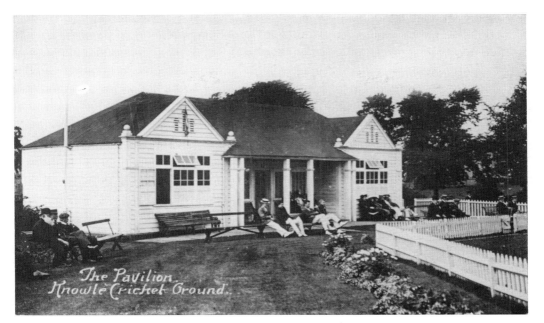

73. The Knowle Cricket Pavilion, players relaxing while waiting for their innings, mingling with spectators. The road immediately behind the Pavilion is Kingshill Road in Knowle Park.

74. The Knowle Cricket Ground in 1923, this view from Wells Road, bordered by Broad Walk behind the trees.

75. The Knowle Hotel in Leighton Road. The Stanton Drew Hunt, meeting at the hotel in 1924.

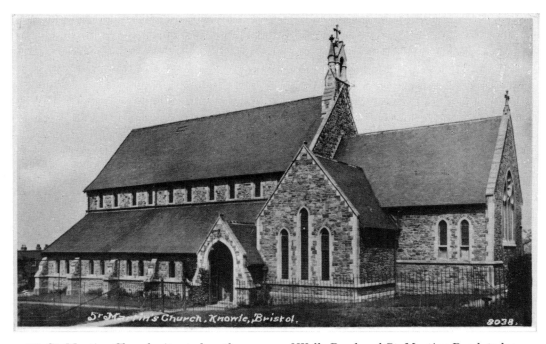

76. St. Martins Church situated on the corner of Wells Road and St. Martins Road, today surrounded by trees and sheltered accommodation flats.

KNOWLE

77. This view looking towards Red Lion Hill in 1916 is still recognisable today with the large houses on the left by the turning for St. Martins Road. Tram No. 70 is passing the unchanged cottages. The Gaiety cinema now stands on the corner on the right hand side of the picture.

78. The Red Lion Inn, in 1906, at the top of the hill which is named after it. Opposite the Inn, Greenleaze and Broadfield Roads. Note the cart parked outside with two large milk churns, the milkman on his deliveries, or gone in for a "Quick Cuppa!".

79. Two trams at the terminus at the top of Red Lion Hill. The Inn of that name and two large double bay houses can be seen behind the trams. Both trams are advertising Andersons Rubber Co. whose premises were in Stokes Croft.

80. Tram No. 169 about to leave the terminus in July 1938. The fields in the background lead towards Whitchurch Village. Today the houses of Hengrove and Whitchurch are built on these fields.

KNOWLE

CROMPTON High Wattage Lamps.in use at the Knowle Greyhound and Speedway Stadium

81. An advertising postcard by Crompton High Wattage Lamps, showing a night time view of Knowle Greyhound and Speedway stadium. The track was situated off of Hengrove Lane, just up from the Happy Landings Inn. today the houses in the area of Petherton Road and Ravenhead Drive have been built on the ground.

82. Mike Beddoe was a very popular member of the Bristol Bulldogs Speedway Team, captained by Billy Hole, in 1947. Knowle Stadium was their home track.

KNOWLE

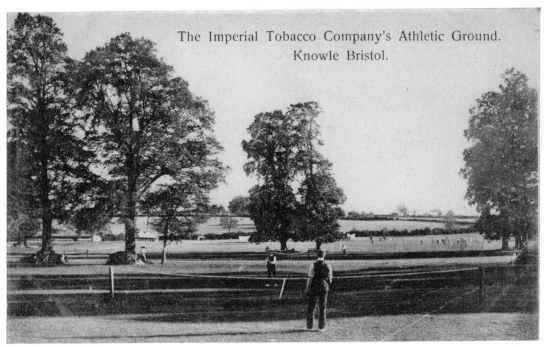

The Imperial Tobacco Company's Athletic Ground.
Knowle Bristol.

83. W.D. & H.O. Wills the Imperial Tobacco Company, had factories in Bedminster and Ashton in Bristol. Their Athletic Ground at the bottom of Red Lion Hill on the Wells Road was bordered by Wotton Park and West Town Lane.

Knowle, Bristol.

84. Looking towards Red Lion Hill from Whitchurch in about 1905. Only a few houses at the top of the hill in Knowle. The Imperial Sports Ground was established in later years, approximately behind the trees centre right.

INDEX